Psychic

I0447524

It's Meaning and History. Are You Psychic or Have ESP? How Can You Develop Your Abilities.

Table of Contents

Introduction

The book is for the individuals who are seeking how to type books to discover their natural Clairvoyance and ESP skills. With the help of the book, you will discover the world of clairvoyance, psychic abilities, visions and how you can get to see the invisible by enhancing your innate clairvoyant abilities.

Anyone interested in learning about psychic development and discovering their own psychic abilities will be able to enjoy this book. Contrary to popular believe, everyone has some psychic ability. Unfortunately, some people don't know how to tap into this limitless power and only certain people are lucky enough to discover it, become aware of it.

Once you have accepted that you have these special psychic abilities and begin to unearth them, you will start to enjoy life fully. The information in this book can be implemented and help you understand and master your psychic intuition better. Whether a novice or a practicing expert studing for years, this book will reveal things you never thought possible. Clearly written, the book will explain to you step-by-step exactly how to unleash your psychic abilities.

The guide is designed for all people in this new brave age of the 21st century who want to go on a journey of self-discovery and self-empowerment. An improvement in your clairvoyance and psychic ability will have a huge helpful impact on your career, relationships, and creativity. This book can help you with all of that. Psychic gifts are safe, spiritual, ethical and essential part of you that makes you whole.

Chapter 1 Clairvoyance and Its History

What is Clairvoyance?

Clairvoyance is the ability to "see" beyond our normal senses into the world of spiritual energy. Clairvoyance literally means "clear seeing". It means seeing a mental image within your third eye, not with your physical eyes. It is also known as your spiritual sight or 6th sense. Clairvoyance is the most recognized, yet least understood intuitive gift on our list of psychic abilities.

A person who has clairvoyance ability is known as a clairvoyant. Clairvoyance permits clairvoyants to see look into the past, present and future to aid people. Clairvoyance has existed for thousands of years. People with clairvoyance ability has used it to guide and advise people about their futures and resolve issues related to the past.

We are all born with clairvoyance ability. During childhood, we have imaginary friends, often see colors or images, and can tell when someone is not being truthful. Clairvoyants don't always have a third eye vision. Occasionally they will have a vision that is similar to watching a movie inside their mind. Other times they might see an image in their mind's eye.

In the physical world, we receive information in many different ways. For instance, if I wanted you to invite a party, I could:

- Text you

- Send you an email

- Call you on your cell phone

No matter which way I invite you, you will get informed about the party. It is same with the intuitive gifts. You can receive psychic messages in various ways.

Anyone, including you, can learn how to tap in and strengthen their intuitive gifts. There are basically four major types of intuitive abilities:

- Clairvoyance or clear seeing: As discussed before, it is the most well known intuitive gift of our psychic abilities. The ability is similar to watching a little movie inside your head. Remember, someone who is clairvoyant is not necessarily having a dramatic psychic vision or seeing the future, similar to what they show in the movies. In real life, clairvoyance can be very subtle. For example, you may just see a symbol, a number or a color. You may or may not fully understand what these symbols or images mean, Other times, you may get a full blown premonition.

- Clairsentience or clear feeling: Clairsentience is the ability to receive intuitive messages via emotions, feelings or physical sensations.

- Clairaudience or clear hearing: clairaudience is a way of receiving intuitive messages with your mind's ears, without using your physical ears.

- Claircognizance or clear knowing: Claircognizance is the ability to just know about something without any facts or logic.

History of Clairvoyance

The history of clairvoyance goes back to biblical times. Abraham, Jacob, and Daniel all had prophetic visions in the Old Testament. In the New Testament, Peter, James, and John "saw" a kingdom of God coming to the earth. For many centuries, the ability to see things with the mind's eye was seen as messages from God. Many consider John – the author of "The Book of Revelations" the first true clairvoyant in history. Although clairvoyance has never been solely a Christian phenomenon. Ancient Hindu religious texts describe a skill that can be achieved through meditation and personal discipline.

Some of the celebrated individual who were famous for their clairvoyance abilities.

- Joan of Arc (1412-1431): The Maid of Orleans or the Joan of Arc had clairvoyant visions that help the teenager lead the French army to defeat the English. Her clairvoyant and leadership ability makes her one of France's greatest heroes.

- Nostradamus (1503-1566): No clairvoyance conversation is not complete without discussing the most famous clairvoyant the world has even known, Nostradamus. Nostradamus clairvoyance visions include The Great fire of London, the French Revolution, Rise of Napoleon and Adolf Hitler, Second World War and yes, 9/11.

- Edward Cayce (1877-1945): Edward Cayce was the most famous clairvoyant of the 20th Century. The deaths of two American Presidents, the rise and fall of Hitler and the prediction about the Soviet Empire among his top predictions.

Parapsychology

For centuries, clairvoyants remained quiet and hidden for fear of being condemned as a witch. The study of clairvoyance started with the Marquis de Puysegur, who was a disciple of Franz Mesmer. In 1784, Franz Mesmer documented a local peasant who was able to see people, places, and events that he could have no knowledge of. Essentially, this was the birth of parapsychology.

In 1931 Duke University researcher JB Rhine developed a standardized methodology for clairvoyance with his "Zener cards". More recently, the Stanford Research Institute has created the term remote viewing and conducted studies into whether people could identify and describe remote targets or locations.

Chapter 2 ESP and Developing Your Psychic Abilities

Have you got ESP?

ESP or Extra Sensory Perception basically refers to our sixth sense. Our five senses are feeling, seeing, hearing, smelling and testing. These are our normal senses, but when a person develops their ESP, they increase their mind's power exponentially. Most of us use it instinctively on a daily basis, but because our minds are so distracted with day to day activities, that we are often oblivious that we process this ability or not. We all possess ESP ability and the ESP power varies amongst individuals.

There are various degrees of ESP. The first step to discovering your ESP abilities is to recognize it, the more you become aware of it the more you are able to develop it and utilize it. Here are some examples often occur to individuals on a daily basis:

- Predicting a future event, such as sport.

- Sensing that someone is ill or depressed without any apparent signs.

- Knowing when the phone is going to ring and who is going to call.

- Sensing that someone is lying, although they do not appear to be.

- Knowing about an event or a newspaper article that will appear in tomorrow's paper.

- Sensing that you will come into contact with a person from the past.

- Predicting a horse to win at a certain race.

- Knowing that someone will have a minor accident or fall.

ESP is mental telepathy

By using their ESP abilities, some people can predict future events about themselves and others. Often they will use some of the following simple exercises:

- Sensing a person's emotion

- Uttering a phrase or a word that someone is thinking

- Accurately identifying simple words that have been written on a sheet of paper

- Use ESP cards which contain symbols such as wavy lines, square, and circle to accurately name the cards.

It's often noticed that people who are lacking one of the primary five senses have the enhanced ability to use ESP. You might have seen a person how have enhanced 6th sense ability. Often people try to hide their true feelings or emotions.
Mothers are good examples of ESP ability. Usually, they instinctively know when their child is in trouble or feeling sick without any of the obvious physical symptoms.
The internet is a great help to know how powerful you ESP really is. Just search online and take some tests.

The Difference Between Psychic and Intuition

People often think that the words 'psychic' and 'intuition' are interchangeable. Both are very closely linked, but there is actually a difference.

Intuition

Intuition is basically a hunch or a border feeling. A feeling towards a particular direction which often can't be logically explained. People describe to this as a hunch or just a feeling or as a gut instinct. A really simple example: your first impression when you meet a person for the first time. Your gut instinct tells you to like or trust them or not. Some of us think that their intuition is their inner voice or a part of them that is connected to something bigger than them. Its voice becomes clearer when you are quiet and still.

Psychic

Being psychic, also called is being clairvoyant. It means that you can identify or receive information that cannot be perceived through your normal five senses. Psychic ability is actually more detailed intuitive information. With more, specific detail, it builds upon your intuition and gives you more clarity and insight about an event or a person. This information may be provided through clairsentience, clairvoyance, clairaudience, clairgustiance or claircognizance. For instance, you meet a stranger and see an image in your mind's eye or instantly feel or know a particular detail concerning their life – this ability is a psychic ability.

Developing your Psychic Abilities

Just like a musical instrument or a difficult sport, psychic ability requires diligent practice. However, unlike music or sport, your progress can be hard to measure because of the elusive nature of psychic phenomena. Usually, it is difficult to know how or when it's going to work. So the frustration level can be high with the practitioners, but just like any other thing, the key to success is patience. There are no guarantees that you will be able to develop your psychic ability, but if you don't try, you are guaranteed not to get anywhere.

Learning how to develop psychic ability is easier than you think. The more you practice, the easier it becomes. Now we are going to discuss strengthening your:

- Clairaudience

- Clairvoyance

- Clairsentience

These exercises are simple, but important steps towards expanding your gift. These exercises are essential because they strengthen your ability to receive intuitive information.

Psychic development exercises for clairsentience

As you know, clairsentience is a way of receiving intuitive information through feelings.

Psychometry

Practice psychometry is a great and fun way to increase your clairsentience. It is about knowing an object by touching it and reading the energy on it. Here is the exercise:

1. For your practice, asks someone to bring you a few small objects that fit in your hands. A metal object such as used keys or jewelry such as a ring is great for practice.

2. Sit comfortably and take a few deep breaths. Then rub your hands together a few times to get the energy circulated. Don't worry if you feel a tingling sensation in your hands.

3. Now take the object in your hands and close your eyes. Carry on relaxing and notice how your body feels. Do you feel, see or hear anything? If not, then it's OK. If you feel you are not progressing with you exercise, ask a few questions to yourself, such as:

   - How is the owner of this object? A man or a woman?

   - Is the owner is currently happy or sad?

   - What is the profession of this person?

   - Does this person have any children?

4. Even if it seems silly, write down everything you feel, see or hear. Don't exclude anything. This exercise will make you familiar with receiving energetic impressions. Share your impressions with your partner, if you are working with any.

5. Finish you practice. Get feedback from the person who gave you the object. Ask if they can validate the things you hear, saw or felt.

This is a great practice and helps you to get used to sensing and reading energy.

Hide and Seek

For this practice, take an object that has a lot of energy, like one of your used clothes or your keys. Ask one of your friends to hide the object and then go outside while they hide it.

Come inside once the object is hidden. Now see if you can connect with the item and feel where it is located. Ask yourself questions such as:

- Is it upstairs or on the first floor?

- Is it placed on top of something or hidden under something?

- Is it in the bathroom, bedroom or in the kitchen, etc?

To find the item, imagine you are connecting with the energy of the item.

Exercise to develop your clairvoyance

Simple visualization exercises can strengthen your clairvoyance.

Tray

1. Ask a friend to place five objects on a flat surface or on a tray. The items should be different from each other. Preferably, these items are completely new to you (unseen to you).

2. Study the objects for about 10 seconds, then ask your friend to remove the objects from view.

3. Imagine each object and picture where it was on the tray. Successfully visualizing these objects in your mind is the key to this exercise. In your mind's eye, recall as many items as you can. With more detail, the exercise is more beneficial. For example, if there was a small notebook on the tray, try to remember the color, the cover, the leather quality and type of paper that was used to make it.

4. Continue to practice daily and as the exercise gets easier, make the exercise tougher for you by adding more objects (10 or 15) and reducing the observation time by half.

Develop your clairaudience ability

Starting to listen is the best way to develop your clairaudience ability. Be aware of the individual and distinct sounds around you.

Here are some tips for improving your clairaudience ability

- Use your occasional idle time. For example, you are waiting in the car for your kids to get out of the school. Use this time to improve your clairaudience ability. Listen: other kids talking as they come out of the school one by one. Parents talking to each other. Other cars driving by. Maybe you can hear the birds if you listen closely.

- While waiting at your doctor's office, listen to the sounds of the office. Listen to the sound of people collecting their serial number from the assistant. The writing on the paper. The typing on the keyboard. Printing sound.

Whenever you have a few moments, do this exercise. After some time, you will be amazed how strong your auditory abilities become. Practicing these exercises are easy and fun. Practice one by one and don't start to practice everything right away.

A step-by-step clairvoyance meditation to open your inner eye or third eye

If you want to open your third eye, then clairvoyance meditation is key. Visualization is the core of this exercise. If you are a visual person, this psychic development exercise will help strengthen that ability. Simply put, you can see a tree in your mind's eye, when you want to. Patience is the key, so don't get discouraged if you don't have a great experience the first time you practice this meditation. The exercise:

- Make yourself comfortable: Go to a quiet place and sit comfortably, relax for a few minutes. But remember, sitting in an upright position is not necessary, lie down or sit, whichever make you comfortable.

- Breathe: Close your eye and take some gentle, deep breaths. Breathe properly, breathe in through your nose and out through your mouth. Place your hands on your belly. Feel your belly expanding when you breathe in and shrinking when you breathe out.

- Begin your third eye meditation: With your eyes closed, visualize the number one with your mind's eyes. The details such as the color or the size of the number don't matter, just focus on seeing the number one in your mind.

- Don't worry, if you feel a tickling sensation in your forehead between your eyebrows. This is where the third eye chakra is located, so the sensation is completely normal. It is OK too if you don't feel anything. With practice, you will feel something. If you find it hard to concentrate, take deep breaths and redirect your focus to what you were doing.

- Continue: Once you can see the number one in your mind, hold the image in your mind for a few seconds. Once you mastered this, then move on to number two, then three, to number ten. Once you can close your eyes and easily visualize the numbers 1 to 10 in sequence, then you have mastered this stage of the exercise.

- If you are struggling: If you are struggling to see through your third eye, give this a try: on a piece of paper, write down the number one and mark is to resemble prominent, such as write it with a marker. Then stare at the image for 20-30 seconds. Now close your eyes and see if you can now visualize the prominent image. People find this trick very useful.

- Moving forward: Once you have mastered the numbers, move on to other objects such as flowers, colors, or anything else you like to visualize.

The practice is really simple and easy and it takes only take a few minutes of daily practice to open your third eye. Start with 2 or 3 minutes and gradually increase your time.

Chapter 3 Types of Psychic Ability and Living with Your Psychic Ability

The following slit of psychic abilities makes up the complete categories of psychic ability. Some psychic say they have only one ability, while other psychics claim that they have several.

- Astral travel or Astral Projection: It is the ability to cause your conscious awareness to be in a position outside of your physical body. This ability is a type of out-of-body experience that assumes the existence of an "astral body" separate from the physical body and capable of traveling outside it. Unlike dreaming or near-death experiences, astral projection is experienced deliberately. Those who experience this phenomenon later describe that seeing their body on an operating table and watching things happening. Some experiencers wake up later and describe events accurately.

- Aura Reading: Reading auras is a very common psychic ability. The aura is a set of cascading colored outlines coming from the surface of the body which differs from person to person in terms of the intensity, color, shape and size. Every living being emanates these energy fields and even lifeless objects have an aura.

- Automatic writing: It is a method that often clairvoyants use to relay information from the spiritual world through their subconscious mind and into written words on the paper. Automatic writing is one method that psychics can use to bring out their psychic energy and describe it to others. The concept behind this ability is that the psychic's hand is eventually controlled by the external intelligence.

- Animal Telepathy: The ability is also called "pet psychics". It is the ability to communicate telepathically with animals. Some people believe that animal trainers often have telepathic communication without realizing it.

- Channeling: This ability is similar to automatic writing. The difference is, instead of controlling psychic's hand, the external spiritual intelligence takes over the vocal chords of the psychic. Psychics who have this ability are known as "medium or Channeler" because they serve as a vessel, or a medium.

- Clairaudience: The ability to hear sounds or voices that are out of reach of a normal ear, such as sounds or words from spirits, angels or guides or simply the call of a loved one from miles away.

- Clairvoyance: Clairvoyance is the ability to attain information about an event, person, object, location or physical event through means other than the known human senses. This is often called as "second sight" or "remote viewing".

- Clairsentience: Clairsentience is the ability to feel or know information about something without seeing it. Basically, it is the psychic's ability to know about the hidden information.

- Divination: A broad term that includes recognition, fortune telling, prophecy, and other methods used to predict the future. Divination is essentially the psychic's ability to foretell the future. Objects such as runes, tarot cards, Ouija boards, crystal gazing and even reading the tea leaves or palm is included in this ability.

- Dowsing: Dowsing is an act completed to find hidden objects. Dowsing has traditionally been a technique of searching for underground water and oil. However, dowsing isn't just about finding water. Dowsing is a technique of finding objects or answers as indicated by the movement of a device such as a pendulum, hazel branches or dowsing rods.

- Empathy: Often this ability is characterized as "put yourself into another person's shoes". This is the ability to understand or recognize another person's state of mind or emotion. Individuals gifted with this ability often pick up a lot of negative emotions and have trouble discerning their own feeling and energies from others.

- Intuition: As described previously, it is a gut feeling or an instinct.

- Levitation: Levitation is psychic ability to levitate their body above the ground. Often people associate levitation with demonic possession.

- Precognition: This is the psychic's ability to know the future. This particular ability involves attaining specific information about an event, rather than a visual viewing of the future.

- Psychometry: Psychometry is also known as "object reading". This ability enables the psychic to pick up on psychic vibrations or impressions left on an object by someone linked to it. Often this psychic ability is dramatically portrayed in movies and TV shows.

- Pyrokinesis: Pyrokinesis refers to the ability to ignite, move, manage or extinguish the fire using only the mind. When it comes to the mind, anything is possible, although not many real documented cases of this ability exist. Sometimes Pyrokinesis ability involves the ability to control the heat itself.

- Telekinesis (also called psychokinesis): This ability is one of the well-known psychic ability because of various movie and TV shows. Telekinesis is the skill to shake or shift items from one place to another with only mind's power. The power can also mean altering the shape of an object by using the mind's energies such as very familiar bending a spoon by just holding it and concentrating on it.

- Telepathy: It involves mind to mind contract. Telepathy is the psychic's ability to communicate to another person without using physical five senses. The ability is often called as "reading minds". As the name suggests the ability includes knowing what other person is thinking or what someone is going to say before they say it.

Living with your psychic gifts

Living with your psychic ability is pleasing, but at times, it can be stressful. There may be days when you feel overwhelmed and lonely and there may be other days when you feel excitement and enthusiasm.

Accept your gifts

Often people with psychic ability wonder, "why can't I just be normal like everyone else?" This is a good indication that you haven't fully accepted your psychic gift. Ask yourself the following questions if you are having trouble living with your psychic gift:

- Is it because you are afraid that your family, friend, and colleagues will judge you?

- Are you fearful of your psychic ability because they contradict your religious beliefs?

- Are you embraced that other people will judge you and make fun of you?

- Are you hesitant or afraid of having visions or being connected to the spirit world?

- Others don't understand your power and you feel like an outsider.

The above feelings are all normal, so relax and don't worry about them. Remember, most people who had a psychic awakening had to pass this stage just like you.

You should accept that not everyone is going to accept who you are. Some people will:

- Not believe you

- Laugh at you

- Want you to prove yourself

- And even if you prove yourself, they will think you are working with evil forces.

It's not worth trying to convince everyone. Apply the rule "go in one ear and out the other". With time things will get easier.

Chapter 4 Why There is Skepticism About Psychic Ability and Ways to Tell If a Psychic is Real

Why there is skepticism about psychic ability

For many years, psychics have been the target of skeptics. There are several reasons behind it. Obviously, the first reason is there have been many fake psychic scammers throughout history. Often fake psychics use elaborate magic tricks to deceive vulnerable people to make a living. Before blindly believing other people's psychic ability, know that the psychic industry is brimming with con artists and fakes. These fake psychics are responsible for creating the devastating stigma attached with the very world psychic.

The second reason why psychics have become the target of skepticism it that people fear what they can't comprehend or things that seem out of place or strange. People naturally fear what is unknown to them. When a normal person claims that they can attain information that transcends the senses as well as time, naturally it creates fear, confusion, and doubt into others.

When a normal person announces that they process paranormal or supernatural activity; it can make the psychic seem non-human, which can then make them seem scary, fearsome and frightening. When one person demonstrates some spiritual or supernatural ability in front of another person who does not process that ability yet, the non-skilled person has the tendency of feeling defeated and less than the other person. This can result in an immediate defensive reaction of trying to undermine that person's credibility. It is an inherited subconscious act of survival instinct for a person who is trying to defeat the feeling of vulnerability or incompleteness.

The third reason psychics are the target of skepticism is because society is much more reason centered today. Currently, we live in a society that has forgotten or ignorant of the role that both the mind and spirit play in reality. Presently many of us see the world as a static reality that exists separate from the mind. So anything that blends spirit, mind and body are often unacceptable to us.

Many well-respected scientists, research institutes, universities tested extrasensory ability with amazingly conclusive and proof positive results. However, psychic ability does not often respond well to testing under controlled conditions. The main reason for this is the intuitive information is totally undermined by pressure, stress and fear. Unlike experts and professionals in other fields, people expect psyches to be all seeing, all knowing and all feeling. This unrealistic expectation leads to the immediate reaction of wanting to test a psychic.

Remember, psychics, like all people are not immune to self-doubt, insecurity, fear, weakness and occasional mishaps.

Ways to tell if a psychic is real

A real psychic will immediately tell you something relevant to your life at the beginning of your reading. The information will be something that you can instantly identify as your own and extremely relevant. Here are some tips to know if a psychic is real or not:

- Let the psychic do all the talking. It's the psychic's job to give you information, not the other way around. Fake psychic's often fishing for information. If they keep asking you questions that end with "does this mean anything to you? Chances are they are fake. A genuine psychic should be able to say why information is relevant to you.

- A psychic must be truthful and should not suppress any information. The information relates to you and they shouldn't hide it.

- Fake psychics try to make things fit. For example, a psychic told you that they see you are in a relationship. But in reality, you are single. After getting that information they might backtrack and say that they are talking about a previous or a future relationship. Well, most people have at least one previous relationship, so the information is too general.

- A true psychic should not take any sides and inject their own opinion. It's your life and the psychic is not your family member.

- A psychic must be to the point, accurate and specific. You will know a psychic is not a real deal when they are making vague statements that could fit anybody's life. Statements like "you have been through some hard times recently, haven't you?", are too vague because most of the people are facing a hard time recently. As soon as you get acquainted with the psychic, they should give you some information that is specifically relevant to your life, not any random information.

- A real psychic empowers you and helps you to find the best way forward. If a psychic says things such as you have been cursed and the only way to avoid is regular sessions or more money, then you know the psychic is false.

Chapter 5 Government Position on ESP

Do authorities use ESP?

The idea of paranormal or supernatural power has intrigued people for centuries. The earliest government research on ESP was during the Cold War. During that time, rumors surfaced that the Russians were developing an army who process psychic ability. The U.S. military quickly took counter measures and created a program to examine whether paranormal or supernatural power could be useful in military applications.

The program was known as Stargate, examined people with psychic powers to see if their visions and feelings were accurate. The program ended in the mid-1990s with very little success. The CIA then took over the program and consulted with scientists if the program is feasible. The scientists gave a negative answer and the Project Stargate was shut down.

But remember great scientist Einstein's 1935 paper named "EPR Paradox," told us that "psychic power" exists in this world. According to Einstein, 2 particles can be at a great distance from each other and one will react when the other is excited or damaged. Einstein called this mysterious action at a distance "psychic phenomenon".

Psychic uses in police work

There are known cases where people claiming psychic abilities have assisted police in solving crimes, but there is considerable skepticism in regard to the general use of psychics in police work. Many police departments around the world, including Australia, New Zealand, UK and the USA have released official statements stating that they do not regard psychics as useful on cases. Here are some examples:

In Australia

Officially Australian police do not accept assistance from psychics. However, they occasionally accept information contributed by psychics. An anonymous Australian police officer told the press that they consulted with psychics on a few cases.

In the UK

The metropolitan Police acknowledge that in one case in 1965, a psychic played an important role in solving the unsolved disappearance case of Thomas "Ginger" Marks.

In the USA

In the US, no police department reported any instances of a psychic investigator providing information that was more helpful than other information received during the course of a case. Although a former senior investigator for the FBI said that psychics may be used as a last resort tool with caution.

In most countries, when the police have already exhausted all of their usual investigative methods and still haven't solved the case, they occasionally consult with psychics because they have nothing left to lose.

Conclusion

Psychic ability will uncover a new world in front you.

www.ingramcontent.com/pod-product-compliance
Lightning Source LLC
Chambersburg PA
CBHW070251290526
45789CB00004B/1819